YOU HAVE PERMISSION

HOW TO STOP DOING STUFF YOU <u>DON'T</u> WANT TO DO AND START DOING STUFF YOU <u>DO</u> WANT TO DO

MARY SCHILLER

Copyright © 2017 Mary Schiller

All rights reserved.

www.maryschiller.com

ISBN: 1542874904
ISBN-13: 978-1542874908

Dedication

To everyone who wants to follow the calling – or callings – of their heart.

Contents

Acknowledgment   i

Introduction You've Got the Power   1

Chapter 1 Permission Slips   3

Chapter 2 But Not for Me?   9

Chapter 3 You Can Quit   17

Chapter 4 You're Free to Do Anything   22

Chapter 5 You Are Creative   29

Chapter 6 A Series of Amazing Events   36

Chapter 7 But ... But ...   44

Chapter 8 Permission Granted   49

Chapter 9 Tell Me All About It   56

ACKNOWLEDGEMENT

To Rachel, my sweet daughter, who has taught me so much about following my dreams, *thank you*.

INTRODUCTION:
YOU'VE GOT THE POWER

"You have permission."

There is magic in those words.

When we internalize them, those words have so much power. More power than we could use in a hundred lifetimes.

This book is all about what "permission" really is: how it made itself known to me, and how you can have permission, too — even if it seems impossible.

As you read, please take your time. Even though this book is brief and concise, there is a lot packed into these few pages. Read, take a break, and then read some more – and try not to skip ahead, because the book unfolds in a deliberate way to help you get the most from it.

What you'll hear as you read the book will be a message tailored just for you. Because you won't be listening to my voice.

You'll be listening to *yourself*.

And you have permission to do that, starting right now ...

Chapter 1:
Permission Slips

Do you remember when you were in school, you had to have a permission slip to go to the bathroom, to walk through the halls while class was still in session, to go see the nurse — or to do anything outside the norms of the prescribed (and often boring) classroom schedule?

We were indoctrinated early to believe that we required permission.

Permission to go somewhere.

Permission to do something.

Permission to talk to someone.

Permission to color the tree purple instead of green, or to make the sky yellow instead of blue — because that was definitely "outside the lines."

Or permission to not color at all and do something completely different.

Perhaps, even though you're not in school anymore, you still live your life waiting for, looking for, listening for permission.

Permission to do something. To try something. To be something.

Permission to stop doing something. To stop trying something. To stop being something.

Until early 2016, I lived that way, too. I believed that I didn't have permission to do what I really wanted to do in life. It didn't even seem like a possibility to me. Instead, I listened to a bunch of "should's" or "have to's" that rolled through my mind all day long. I didn't see life as being filled with options and choices, nor did I take time to listen to, let alone answer, the callings of my heart. I shoved those desires aside — really,

I snuffed them out at every turn — because they seemed not just irrelevant, but impractical. Frivolous. Only for people whose circumstances allowed them the freedom to live life on their own terms.

And that certainly didn't seem like me. For the first part of my adult life, I was in a violent marriage. When I eventually left that marriage, I was a single parent working several jobs just to keep the bills paid and food in the refrigerator.

Later on, I still put everything and everyone in front of my own dreams — which had become pretty faded over time — because it looked to me like that was simply how things worked. I mean, how else was I supposed to live? Living any other way struck me as selfish.

But then, in a stunning surprise in early 2016, I saw something new. Something that changed everything about how I live my life. I discovered that not only is it a great thing to give yourself permission to do what you want to do in life, but it's also the right thing to do.

All those years up until that point, I had thought giving myself permission to do what I wanted to do in life was the wrong thing to do. And then suddenly, I saw that I, myself, had been wrong.

Why is it good to give ourselves permission?

Because the world needs you — we need everything that you are. So when you don't give yourself permission to listen to what is calling to you, it means that the world is missing out on an amazing gift, or often many gifts, that you can give to us. I want to do something about that. I don't want another day to go by where you don't believe you're allowed to do what you want to do in this life.

Fair warning, though. This book may not be what you think it is. In fact, I'm pretty sure it isn't. But that may be a really good thing, so I invite you to read some more and see if you agree. If you're looking for a book that will give you lots of personality inventory tests that lead you to a series of letters, numbers or colors that describe you, then this is not the book for you. (I don't believe human beings can be reduced to a bunch of symbols, do you?)

If you're looking for a book that will tell you what type of work or hobby suits you based on a list of checkboxes, then this is not the book for you. (It's fun to take quizzes, but this book is a lot more profound than that — even though it's just as simple to understand as a magazine quiz.)

If you're looking for a book that will help you find your life purpose, then this is not the book for you. (Aren't there enough of those books already? I thought so, too, which is why I didn't write one. And besides, what you'll find here is even better!)

If, however, you're looking for a book that will show you a simple way to experience the most incredible feeling of freedom — freedom to pursue your interests, or even the freedom to discover your interests for the first time — then I invite you to keep reading.

As I am writing this paragraph right now, tears are streaming down my face. If I had had one significant person in my life — just one — give me permission to have my own dreams, follow my instincts, and even set aside what looked like obligations and listen to my heart, I would have been able to spend more years pursuing the things that I really loved to do in life.

Not only that, the world might have been given the best version of Mary, the one who could have contributed to the greater good in ways I can't even imagine.

That's what I want for you. And no matter what your circumstances may be or how old you are — I'm 55 right now, in 2017 — it's not too late. I want to be the person who gives you permission: permission to stop doing stuff you don't want to be doing anymore, and start doing stuff you really do want to do.

To begin, I'd like to take you behind the scenes as to why the notion of "permission," and my desire to have you experience it, has become such a focal point of my life. Let's rewind the clock a bit (or more than a bit) to the 1960s …

Pause for Reflection

- Permission slips may have been needed in school, but they're not required to live the life you really want to live.
- If you're waiting for someone else to give you permission, you may wait forever (unless you include me, in which case, the wait is over!)

Chapter 2:
But Not for Me?

In this chapter, I'll show you why the notion of "permission" was such a foreign concept to me – as it might be for you right now, too. Our stories will be different, but you may recognize yourself in what you read in this chapter.

When I was growing up in the 1960s and '70s, my parents weren't at all inquisitive about what I might want to do in life. The proverbial question of "What do you want to be when you grow up?" was absent from my childhood, at least from my parents. My life situation was a bit odd, too, in that I came along very late in the family. My brother was 16 and my sister, already out of the house and in college when I was born, was 19. The three of us kids had the same parents, but clearly there was a big age — and generation — gap. My parents had raised two children in the 1940s and '50s, and when I came along in 1961, I don't think they knew what to do with me.

My father wasn't around much, as he always seemed to be working or traveling. So after my brother moved out, it was just my mom and me. To her credit, my mother did see that I had an interest in music at an early age, so I took piano lessons starting when I was five. I always loved making up stories, too.

I did well in school, and later on, I liked playing tennis and swimming. Even though I was clearly expressing myself through these activities, my parents didn't talk to me about them. My father didn't usually attend my piano recitals, for example, and my parents were completely flabbergasted when I won a prestigious poetry contest. They literally said that they couldn't believe I took first prize.

They weren't bad parents, but they didn't guide me in a specific direction based on my interests, talents and skills.

In my teen years, I began to realize that I was really on my own. I noticed that unlike when I visited my friends' homes, in our house there weren't any dinner table discussions about career choices I might consider. Although I worked part time at my dad's small company when I was in junior high and high school, he didn't share anything about what was involved in running your own business. He taught me how to be a good employee, but nothing more than that.

So when I was thinking about what to study for my undergraduate degree, I selected a major simply based on the fact that I enjoyed it: music. In all honesty, I was not super talented as a pianist, but I didn't want to stop playing because I loved it. I also spent hours and hours with my headphones on and the turntable spinning, listening to music of all kinds. And where I wanted to go to school — the University of California, Los Angeles — the music department offered two years of free instrument lessons to all music majors. That was good enough for me, so I applied.

It wasn't an easy feat to get invited to join the music department at UCLA. Not only did I have to get accepted to the university, but I also had to pass a rigorous music entrance exam and an audition before I could become a music major.

After a lot of study and practice, I passed the tests and the audition and was also accepted to the university. I was in! I was so excited. I loved the UCLA campus, and the music department had a great reputation and excellent piano faculty. I couldn't wait to start this new chapter of my life.

And then, my parents dropped a bomb: They told me that if I majored in music, they wouldn't pay for my college education. Their reasoning was that, in their opinion, I wasn't good enough in music to "make it." I needed to find something more practical to do with my education.

I was crushed. It sounded like they had no faith in me at all, and it also seemed unfair that after offering me no guidance, they suddenly decided that I wasn't capable of directing my own life.

How could they do this to me? I cried and cried ... and then I started taking action. I investigated all the ways I could pay for my education myself. So I gathered all the financial aid paperwork together and showed it to my parents, and I told them I didn't need their money. I would do it myself.

They relented. Begrudgingly, but they relented. (And in case you're wondering, yes, that situation did affect my relationship with my parents — really just with my father, because I believe he pressured my mother into telling me they wouldn't help.)

When I started college, I already knew I wasn't going to be a professional pianist, and I didn't want to do that, anyway. I discovered that I was talented in two areas: music history and music analysis. I also realized that my skills in English, literature and writing were quite high, so I took a lot of extra English classes because I really enjoyed them.

But even so, all through my time at UCLA I didn't know what I was going to do once I graduated. I was still feeling directionless, although I had a great time while I was in college and made wonderful friends. In the back of my mind were always thoughts about not being good enough to be a music major, not being a talented enough writer to win a poetry prize, not being smart or aware enough to choose the best direction for my own life.

After I graduated from UCLA, my life took a dramatic turn. I made an impulsive decision at age 22 to marry a man who turned out to be violent and abusive. I managed to survive and escape that marriage (literally, I fled for my life with my then-two-year-old daughter).

When I got divorced at age 29, I didn't know what to do. I certainly didn't feel free to do what I wanted to do, whatever that might have been. I didn't have time to even consider anything that looked like a desire or dream. As a single mother of a toddler, I had immediate obligations, and I was looking at life solely from a practical point of view. What did I have to do to get the bills paid? How could I keep my daughter safe? My attention was given over to those aspects of life and nothing else.

As I reached my early 30s, I still was seeing life from the vantage point of survival. To improve my chances of getting a better-paying job, I went back to school and earned a master's degree in English. Even though I liked English, pursuing that degree wasn't something I was passionate about — it was solely for the job opportunities I thought it would afford me so that I could be a better provider for my daughter. A few years later, I earned a second master's degree, this one in education, again just for the potential opportunities for career advancement, not out of a real desire to be a teacher. The combination of degrees definitely opened up professional doors for me.

But I was still focused on getting by — in other words, paying the bills, not doing what I wanted to do with my time. I had a few hobbies outside of work, like photography and swimming. And of course, I loved raising my daughter; eventually, I remarried.

Unfortunately, life felt more like existing than living much of the time. I wasn't engaged with life, not in the way that other people seemed to be. For example, many of my college friends had forged great careers for themselves that they really loved: running their own companies, teaching art, investing in real estate, leading a church ministry. When I talked to them, they sounded like they were completely passionate about what they were doing professionally, and that enjoyment spilled over into their personal lives, too.

They were happy and free.

I didn't — couldn't — understand how they felt such freedom in life. I had no conscious awareness of that kind of freedom: the freedom to choose my own path based on what looked like fun, what looked interesting. For me, those days were over, if they ever really existed. Everything had become about surviving, not about pursuing what I wanted to do.

In other words, I thought the notion of "following your dreams" was only for rich people, privileged people, or people who didn't have the same kinds of obligations — and traumatic past — that I had. I lumped my friends into those categories, too. I walked around in a state of jealousy and downright anger much of the time, wishing I had the kind of freedom and happiness that other people enjoyed.

And while that didn't seem fair, it also seemed like a fact. It wasn't fixable. My life simply was what it was, and I had to accept it.

Well, as you might guess based on the title of this book, I couldn't have been more wrong. But I had to learn three essential lessons before I could make the changes I wanted to make — to feel that sense of freedom I longed for. To me, these lessons are crucial, so let's look at the first one together.

Pause for Reflection

- If it seems like everyone else is able to live the life of their dreams but that that couldn't possibly be true for you, allow yourself to imagine that it actually *is* possible.
- Your dreams are there for a reason. They are not frivolous.

Chapter 3:
You Can Quit

On my journey toward giving myself permission (since no one else was doing it for me), I learned three lessons — or you could say that I had three big insights — that were crucial in terms of creating the beautiful new life I'm now living: a life based on what I actually want to be doing instead of what I believe I ought to be doing. In this chapter, I'll share the first lesson with you, which relates to sticking with something until the bitter end.

And I know exactly where that tendency came from ...

My mother had a phrase that she repeated often throughout my childhood: "Finish the job." She would often say say it about doing chores around the house. For example, if I was responsible for cleaning the kitchen after dinner, she would always remind me to "finish the job." What did that mean, exactly? It meant that not only did the dishes need to be in the dishwasher and all the pots and pans washed, dried and put away, but also that the sink was scoured and the sponge was wrung out and set back in its holder by the faucet. It also meant that the counters were wiped down and everything looked as spotless as it could be.

If, for instance, I forgot to scour the sink and instead, I went into the family room to watch TV, my mom would come in and say, "Mary, finish the job" — and I always knew that I had forgotten to scour the sink, and then ring out the sponge (that part was important) and set it into its holder.

Now I don't want to make my mother sound like some kind of meanie, because she wasn't. She was a lovely, and loving, woman. She meant the world to me, and I to her. I think what she was trying to do was instill good habits in me: meaning, don't leave things unfinished. Don't start something and then not follow through — that sort of thing.

My father had a similar outlook. When I was working for his company after school when I was in my teens, I learned that the boss really appreciates it if you go the extra mile to "finish the job." Consequently, I never did anything halfway.

As I grew older, that phrase "finish the job" kept popping up in my head. Unfortunately, it was beginning to become a problem, because it also seemed to indicate to me that I couldn't leave something behind if I didn't like it.

In other words, I believed I wasn't allowed to quit. I had to finish everything I started.

The most poignant example was my first marriage, which, as I mentioned a few paragraphs back, was filled with violence perpetrated by my then-husband. Throughout all of it, in the back of my mind lurked that phrase, "finish the job" — and somehow, I took that to mean that if I had the impetus to leave my marriage, I couldn't. It seemed like I needed to stick it out until the end, even though I wasn't sure what the end was supposed to look like. I had made a commitment; that was it.

I stayed in that marriage far longer than I should have: seven years, all of which were filled with abuse against me and, later, my daughter. I am not blaming my parents for any of that, of course, but I know that the thinking I had about staying until something was finished definitely played a role in my inability to walk away — until I was literally looking at the possibility of being killed.

One day, I saw that possibility staring me in the face, with my then-husband threatening to kill me and/or my mother. He wasn't joking. In a flash, I knew that I had to take my toddler daughter with me and get out, so I made plans as quickly as I could and left just two days later.

While that wasn't the end of the abuse, which continued in various forms for several years through court battles and other things, it was the end of the marriage. Significantly, it was the first time I quit something. And that was, even in the midst of all the trauma and chaos, a truly breakthrough moment for me.

So here is lesson no. 1: You can quit.

Yes, you really can.

You have permission to quit.

Pause here for a moment and let that sentence sink in. You might even close your eyes and allow yourself to breathe quietly, listening for what comes to you when you hear the words, "I have permission to quit." It may take some time for those words to become real to you, and that's quite all right. For now, give yourself permission to entertain the idea that you can — yes, you really can — quit.

As you'll see in the next chapter, quitting can have consequences. But we can never know precisely what those consequences will be (hint: they're not always bad!).

Pause for Reflection

- If you're used to abiding by the phrase "Never give up," start imagining what your life might be like if you had the option to quit. Because you actually do have that option.
- Quitting can be seen as a bad thing, but in actuality, it is neither good nor bad. It is neutral; it's simply a choice.

Chapter 4:
You're Free to Do Anything

If lesson no. 1 — you can quit — revealed itself to me in my late 20s when I left my first marriage, lesson no. 2 waited an awfully long time to show up: 25 years, as a matter of fact. This is a biggie, both for you and for me. So here goes …

In 2015, I found myself stuck in a job that I really didn't like. OK, let's just say it like it was: I hated it.

I had been working as a communications offer for an Ivy League university since 2007, and in actuality, I had completely lost interest in the work in 2009. However, I had committed to staying there through mid-2010 because of the incredible benefits package the university offered, which included paying for my daughter's college tuition. Just as I had done before in other endeavors, like taking certain jobs and going to graduate school, I was not at the university because it appealed to my passions — it didn't at all — but because the job filled a need and helped with an obligation.

When my daughter graduated from college in 2010, I knew that I was then free to leave the university. Her tuition had been paid for, so there was no reason to stay. But I could never seem to actually get out the door and do something else. I started up some freelance writing work on the side, which failed miserably because again, it wasn't something I loved. Instead, it looked more like an exit sign from the university than something fun to pursue.

And harkening back to "finish the job," I often felt confused about when something was actually finished. Even though I was truly unhappy working at the university, I thought that maybe there was some way I could improve it, like fixing my relationship with my boss (who absolutely hated me) or finding a way to make an impact that I hadn't discovered before. But the thing is, the whole time I was in that job, I knew deep down that I was in the wrong place.

Even stranger, as I look back on it now, anytime I had an idea of what else I might do professionally that sounded fun and interesting, I pushed it away or ignored it. None of it seemed possible, practical or doable. That time of my life was emblematic of everything that came before it, consisting of a series of "should's" and "have-to's." I never saw much in the way of choice except that I could choose to be responsible or irresponsible, particularly with work. I always chose what looked like the former: being responsible.

I needed a new way of seeing life.

It showed up in the spring of 2015, while I was on a walk in Central Park in New York City.

At that time, I was still in the communications job for the university, and my office was just a block away from Central Park. Every day, unless the weather was truly awful, I spent my lunch hour walking through the park. Oh, the things I saw on those walks! People playing softball games, tourists taking selfies, New Yorkers walking their dogs and riding bikes, horses pulling the carriages. One time, I saw a sweet mother squirrel moving her tiny, pink-eraser-looking babies to a safer location. With great care, she would hold a baby in her mouth and cross the bike/horse carriage/walking path, drop it into the safer spot, and then run back toward me and repeat the process. Such determination and dedication.

On a beautifully sunny day, I was on the last leg of my walk, having already made the turn back in the direction of my office. Suddenly, I was gripped — it literally felt like something or someone grabbed hold of me — with a new thought: "You don't have to go back there, Mary. You can do whatever you want, today, tomorrow, every day.

"In fact," the thought continued, "you could, if you wanted to, go to the airport right now. You could use your credit card to buy a ticket to somewhere in the U.S., maybe a city you've never visited before. And if you wanted to, you could stay there. Or you could come back or go somewhere else."

I stopped walking and just stood there, under the trees and in a bit of a clearing away from the crowds in the park. If someone had taken a photograph of me in that moment, I'm sure I would have looked somewhat stunned in my expression.

"Wait a minute!" I said to myself. "I can do whatever I want. I can do whatever I want," I repeated.

"But wouldn't there be consequences?" I asked, not sure who or what I was asking, but knowing there would be an answer forthcoming.

"Yes," said the next thought that came to me. "But you don't know what they are. No one can know what they are, even when we think we can."

And then, a waterfall of thoughts rained down on me, like "OK, what if I decided not to pay my taxes? I'm free to not pay my taxes, right?"

The next thought was, "Yes, you're free not to pay your taxes. You might go to jail, but you don't know what the actual consequences might be."

That was huge!

Here I had always believed that if I did what looked like the responsible thing to do, if I met my obligations and so on, that I was guaranteed certain consequences or results. But my life hadn't shown me that at all. Nothing had ever really gone the way I thought it would, even when I took what looked like the "responsible" route.

The same was true for my friends who had followed their passions. They didn't know what the consequences or results would be. But it seemed to me that they had a better chance of success if they were listening to, and responding to, what was calling to them. And as I saw that day in Central Park, that was also true for me.

And it is true for you, too. You have a better chance of succeeding in something you do want to do than in something you don't.

In another thought, I realized that being free to do what I wanted didn't mean that I should act on every single idea that came to me, especially those that involved potentially harming another person. We've all had those thoughts before, and that's not what I'm talking about here, of course.

But what I heard, loud and clear, was ...

Lesson no. 2: You're free to do anything you want.

Anything at all.

You have permission to wake up tomorrow — yes, you really do — and do whatever you want to do.

As before, take some time here to let those words become more real to you: "I'm free to do anything I want."

Pause for Reflection

- It only looks like there are limitations placed on us because we *think* – operative word here – they are real.
- When you are inspired to do something, your chances of making that dream come into reality are much higher than if you're doing things you don't want to do. So for example, if you want to change the way you earn money – leave a dead-end job and do what you enjoy – you're more likely to succeed in doing what you enjoy. I'll talk more about this later in the book, so stay tuned for the wonderful details.

CHAPTER 5:
YOU ARE CREATIVE

You've now seen the first two lessons — or insights — related to giving ourselves permission:

Lesson no. 1: You can quit.

Lesson no. 2: You're free to do anything you want to do.

The third lesson I learned — the third major insight I had — was absolutely indispensable to create a life I truly wanted to be living. Even though I already had those first two insights, I wasn't fully experiencing them. It was the combination of those plus the third one that made all the difference. I'm sure it will do the same for you, so let's pick up our story ...

In the late spring of 2015, I took a freelance job as an editor with a small startup, something to do in addition to my role at the university (where I was still feeling stuck). A few months later, to my surprise the two startup founders offered me a full-time job, and I finally left the university.

But once again, I did so only because the startup looked like a good opportunity to make more money and also work from home, since there was no central office and everyone worked remotely. I wasn't really interested in the business itself, and on top of that, I had to turn a blind eye to the personality and antics of the CEO, someone I didn't respect or like very much. But I gave him, and the job, the benefit of the doubt — even though at times, the small voice inside my head and heart got quite loud, saying, "Don't take this job!"

Talk about not listening to myself or my intuition. Yikes! I did just the opposite, ignoring everything I heard within me and, instead, looking toward what seemed to be demanded of me: a way to support my family that afforded me more flexibility and the possibility of a windfall, money-wise.

Can you guess what happened?

You Have Permission: How to Stop Doing Stuff You Don't Want to Do and Start Doing Stuff You Do Want to Do

On my very first day, I knew 100 percent that I had made a terrible mistake. I discovered that during the hiring process, the CEO — the one to whom I had given the benefit of the doubt — had not informed me of something so critical, that had I know it earlier, it would have stopped me from accepting the position. I had been conned: a bait-and-switch situation.

Instead of following the voice I heard inside me in that moment saying, "Mary, you can still quit right now!" I decided to stick it out. I tried, as I learned at a young age, to "finish the job"— mostly because at the time, I was the sole breadwinner and felt I had no other option. It was either stay in that job or get sent to the poor house, is how it looked to me.

So I threw everything that I had into the startup role and was determined to make the best of the situation.

Six months later, I decided to share my concerns with the CEO directly. He was someone who said he always wanted us to tell him the truth, especially if we saw him making a possible mistake. You may not be shocked to learn that he fired me — and at a most inopportune time. My husband was still not working due to a family crisis, and we had just spent almost all of our savings on some emergency repairs to our home

So there I was, having made decisions that did not feel like they were coming from my heart, but instead from some sense of duty: all about getting the bills paid and taking care of other people's needs.

And this time, I had nothing tangible to show for it. Almost no cash left, no job, no prospects and mounting credit card debt. I was completely freaked out, embarrassed and scared, and I didn't know what to do. Fortunately, someone was there to listen to me in that moment of crisis.

I called a life coach I had spoken to a few times before. Looking back on that conversation now, I can imagine that I sounded like I was out of my mind. I know that I was crying, and I couldn't remember feeling that frightened in a long time. I was on the verge of complete financial collapse, and my life looked like an either-or scenario: Either I fix this situation right now, or my world is going to completely fall apart, and me along with it.

As we talked, the coach's actual words started to fade into the background, and into the foreground emerged a feeling of peace and well-being. First, I saw that I wasn't experiencing a lack of money or getting fired, but my own thinking. So I had the option to not listen to that thinking if I didn't want to. That small shift helped a lot., and ignoring that freaked-out thinking helped me hear another major insight.

I'll never forget this moment for as long as I live.

I hung up the Skype call with the coach, and I sat there, looking out the window of the apartment I lived in at the time, in the Bronx in New York City. It was the end of January of 2016, and the winter was in full swing: barren trees, gray skies and a hint of snow on the ground. As I took in the view — which really wasn't much to look at — I heard a new thought.

"You already have everything you need, Mary."

I sat in stunned silence for a few moments, and then I began to cry again. Because that insight wasn't just about the fact that I was sitting in a warm apartment, with food in the refrigerator and clothes in the closet. It was about a whole lot more than that.

It was telling me that I had everything I needed to create the life I really wanted to be living, just by virtue of being human – by virtue of being alive.

I, like you, have been given a gift simply by being born: innate and infinite creative resources.

Life is not an either-or proposition, ever (even when it looks like it is). In that moment, I saw that not only did I have infinite possibilities laid out before me like a beautiful buffet, but that those infinite possibilities were part of me. In essence, I *was* those possibilities. I was infinitely creative, in and of myself. Not in an artistic sense, but in a "creating life" sense. I had already been creating a life for myself; it just wasn't the one I really wanted to be living. All I had to do to change it was realize that I had the option to do so.

I could ignore the dark and scary thoughts, and in their place would arise this innate creativity, filled with possibility and choice. The bleak thoughts lifted all on their own, and I saw ...

Lesson no. 3: You are innately and infinitely creative.

You have permission to access this infinite well of creativity to help you — much more effortlessly — to do what you want to do in life. How? Allow any thoughts to the contrary to pass on by without giving them so much attention, and start noticing how creativity shows up for you every single day. I'll talk more about this, coming up shortly.

And in the next chapter, I'll share what happened once all three of these lessons came together ...

Pause for Reflection

- Your life isn't just full of possibilities. Those infinite possibilities are actually *who you are*.
- Allow yourself to sit with the truth that you already have everything you need and you always will, no matter how your circumstances may change.

CHAPTER 6:
A SERIES OF AMAZING EVENTS

I have been astonished by what has occurred in my life – and more importantly, in the way I experience my life – since having those three big insights. In this chapter, I'll share a few examples to give you some concrete ideas of what is possible and how quickly things can change …

At the end of January 2016, I was jobless and nearly broke, cash-wise. My husband wasn't working at the time because, as I alluded to earlier, he was dealing with something major — the illness and approaching death of his father. He had to quit his job so that he could be in California with his dad (his employer wouldn't let him telecommute), and we hadn't counted on my being fired from my job. Our credit card debt was already climbing, and I was trying to keep us afloat.

But — and this is a BIG "but" — I had just had that breakthrough insight, which I've called Lesson no. 3: You are innately and infinitely creative.

In moments of peace among the times of stress that first part of the new year, I had a strong sense that things were going to be different somehow. I didn't know what else would change besides losing my job at the startup, but something was going to happen — I was certain of it.

And then, the first of four amazing events occurred.

First Amazing Event: The CEO — the person who fired me — came back to me and offered me a month's severance pay, saying that he would check in with me at the end of February to see how I was doing.

Wow! I couldn't believe it. That was four weeks where I could consider my next steps and truly ignore any stressful thinking I had about money and getting the bills paid. So during February, I wrote a little book, which I titled *The Joy Formula*. A few months earlier, I had started a daily audio blog just for fun, called The Daily Principles, so I put *The Joy Formula* on the website as a gift if people subscribed to my email list. The feedback I received on the book, which at that time was a .pdf, was really positive. I had been coaching people off and on — all for free — for a couple of years, and I began to wonder, "Could I actually make a living coaching people and writing books?"

Second Amazing Event: At the end of February 2016, one month after he had fired me, the CEO offered me another month's severance pay — even more time to take a breather, knowing I could cover my mortgage payment and the other financial obligations at least in the short term. Double wow! I was home free until the end of March.

Suddenly, I began to see more light in my life: as if some unseen force, a creative force, was trying to help me change direction. I still didn't know exactly what that direction was, but I was willing to wait for it to appear.

As April approached and my second month of severance pay was running low, my husband was still with his ailing father, so he wasn't working yet, either.

Then … the Third Amazing Event happened: I did something completely and totally new that changed the course of my life forever. And when I say "forever," I mean it. This was major.

As I mentioned a moment ago, I had been coaching people — really just having conversations — for free or nearly free for quite some time. I didn't consider myself a professional coach at all. In fact, I hadn't even received any coach training or certification. I had simply been inspired to help people. As weird as this sounds to me now, I never thought my services were worth charging for.

Until, in a flash, I did. What I heard inside me was, "You can start charging, Mary. Right now." As I sat in my little Bronx apartment contemplating what I'd just heard, I took that phrase even further. I began to cry, with deep sobs of joy, as I gave myself permission …

- To quit chasing after money as a way to feel secure because I realized that security is innate, not something I get from anything "out there."

- To do what I really wanted to do, which was work for myself in a way that also helps others.

- To access, with more joy and trust, the innate creativity that was given to me the moment I came into this world, so I could have the life I really wanted to be living.

Once I *gave myself permission*, it was like the floodgates opened. And then came ...

The Fourth Amazing Event: I created a profitable business really fast — literally within one month. The first month I started charging for my coaching, I met my monthly goal of $5,000. And I've met or exceeded that goal every month since then. Not only that, but — and this is the truly astonishing part — in the past nine months, I have met, talked to, worked with and/or been interviewed by the leading people in my particular coaching field.

As I'm writing this paragraph, also in the last nine months I've written and self-published four more books in addition to *The Joy Formula*, traveled to Norway for a wonderful conference, partnered with another coach on a new business, sold my husband's and my apartment in the Bronx and am making plans to move permanently to Paris, France, in early 2017 — that last part being a dream I've had since I was 20 years old.

You Have Permission: How to Stop Doing Stuff You Don't Want to Do and Start Doing Stuff You Do Want to Do

How did all of this happen?

Simple.

I gave myself permission.

Permission to quit doing stuff I didn't want to do.

Permission to do what I actually wanted to do.

Permission to listen to the creativity within me — the creativity that *is* me — and allow it to flow out into the world in brand new and exciting ways.

Here's something important: Anytime I had a thought that said, "Mary, you can't do that," I gave myself permission to ignore it. I didn't try to stop those thoughts or change them. I just ignored them and watched them float on by. If they brought with them a feeling of anxiety or stress, I ignored that, too, and just went about my business!

I knew I didn't need to worry about whatever feeling I had, because it was all coming from momentary thought. Worry or fear didn't tell me anything substantive about what was doing;

it reflected only what thoughts were going through my head, and they would change without my doing anything about them.

By giving myself permission and ignoring thoughts and feelings that told me anything different, I allowed all of that innate creativity, that infinite well of possibility, to flood into and then through me. As a result, the new ideas and the actions I took were much more inspired and leveraged, and my stress level was near zero — so my ability to accomplish goals I set for myself was enhanced a thousand fold.

Was 2016 a "perfect" year? No. My father-in-law passed away, and my family and I felt his death as a tremendous loss. Did I hit every financial goal I set? No. As I'm writing this book, my husband and I are still clearing away our debt.

But in terms of experiencing a completely different way of living, one filled with freedom, success, creativity, magic and joy? I can't remember another year like it.

Now that I know that I have permission to listen to what's calling to me, and to follow the dreams that had once been a distant memory but now appear in vivid, living color right before my eyes, everything has changed for the better. My relationships, my friendships, my health, my daily experience, my professional life — everything has improved dramatically.

In the next chapter, you and I will start to look at what having permission can mean for your life. I'm ready! Are you? Then let's go ...

Pause for Reflection

- You are allowed to simply ignore any thoughts you have that you don't like or that bring a bad feeling. Don't try to change them (because you actually can't). Those thoughts and feelings will change on their own in a moment, so wait them out and listen for what appears in their place.
- Your own series of amazing events is already unfolding, perhaps starting with reading this book.

CHAPTER 7:
BUT ... BUT ...

You: "Objection!"

Me: "Overruled!"

Before we look at how granting yourself permission can make a huge impact on your life, I want to address your objections. I know you have them, because I can practically hear them from here, like ... "But Mary, you don't understand my circumstances. I can't just drop everything to do the things I want to do. I have responsibilities. Commitments. Obligations. People to support. Mouths to feed. What would happen if I just forgot about all of that and pursued my dreams? It would spell disaster, Mary!"

I had all those thoughts, too. Every single one, and then some. They were screaming — loudly — in my head most of my waking hours for years. Yes, years. When I finally gave myself permission in 2016 to make a different decision, to ignore those thoughts and go in a different direction based on the callings of my heart, I was as skeptical as anyone whether things would really change for the better.

I realized with absolute astonishment and delight that obstacles began to disappear: things that had really looked solid, like a lack of money, for example. Why? Because they were figments of my imagination. Oh, wait! I can hear you now: "But Mary, these kids I have aren't figments of my imagination. Neither is my spouse or my job. People expect things from me."

I get it. I really do. As I mentioned earlier, I was a single mother for many years. I have had my own struggles like with post-traumatic stress disorder, for instance. But if you really listen to what I'm saying in this book — meaning, listen to the voice within you that's speaking to you as you read — you'll hear that circumstances can't stop you from doing what you want to do. Only thoughts can do that. And you're not obligated to listen to your thinking, especially when it gets loud and obnoxious. That's when you know for certain that you can ignore it, because it's not telling you the truth. The volume level will get turned down on its own, and those thoughts will fade into the background – and truth will emerge.

The truth is found in your innate capacity for creativity and expansion, for change and growth. That voice you hear that says, "I'd really love to …" is telling you to do something you're already equipped to do. Otherwise, you wouldn't be hearing it. It's amazing what can happen when you take one simple step in the direction of things that appeal to you. Life with a capital "L" will step up to help you. New ways of taking care of obligations will become obvious. Time will start to seem less rigid and more fluid, and your productivity will increase without effort.

But what about finding our "life purpose"?

I'd like to revisit this notion that people have a "life purpose," and that unless we find that one thing we're destined to do with our lives, we're doomed to live a life "less than." I was lost in that kind of conversation for many years, feeling ashamed that I didn't have a "life purpose." You'll remember I mentioned my friends who seemed to find that special thing in their lives and how much I envied them. But you know what I have to say to that notion of "life purpose" today? I think it's bull pucky.

What I really wanted wasn't to find my life purpose. No, what I really wanted — and what I suspect you want — is to have a life of freedom: freedom to try things, to experiment, to listen to the voice inside and act from its inspiration. I don't believe that we are such singular beings as to have one thing that we are supposed to be doing. Yes, there are some people who devote their lives to something, and that's wonderful. But we are also allowed to explore fully our capabilities as human beings — to look at what is really possible and simply go for it.

My daughter is a great example of what we're talking about. She is someone who enjoys many different types of activities, and for a long time, she criticized herself for that. The message we often get from the world is to "focus, focus, focus" — basically, that the only way we'll be successful is to pick something and stick with it (sound familiar?). But as a result of listening to her own voice and following the callings of her heart, at age 28 my daughter has traveled the world and spent extended time in foreign countries, learned to speak another language fluently, enjoyed such diverse activities as competitive rowing and ballroom dancing, and is about to complete her doctorate in order to become a university professor. The reason I'm using her as an example isn't to brag (although I'm certainly proud of her), but to show that whatever we're doing, when we're giving ourselves permission, there is a foundation that underscores everything, something that is available to us in every moment of our lives: freedom.

Freedom … to be this magnificent, creative being that you are already.

Freedom … to do anything you want to do.

Pause for Reflection

- Even when limitations look real, they are not. (You may want to re-read that sentence a few times to let it sink in.) Limitations are thoughts that you're listening to, and you're not obligated to listen to them. They'll fade into the background the less attention you pay to them.
- You're already equipped with everything you need to do what you really want to be doing in life. So start doing it.

CHAPTER 8:
PERMISSION GRANTED

Are you starting to believe that you can do whatever you want to do in this life? It's not just that I'm giving you permission, or that now you're giving yourself permission. It's that life is giving you permission: L-I-F-E.

Did you get that? LIFE wants this for you!

When you have the notion to do something new, even something very different from the norm for you, it means that you have everything you need to do it. You've been given a gift just by being alive: your innate and infinite creativity that I wrote about earlier is there to help you. How do you access that creativity? By giving yourself permission to do what you want to do, and then taking one small step toward doing it.

That simple act is like holding out your hands and allowing creativity and infinite possibilities to pour in and help you create whatever you want to create in your life.

Look around you. Evidence of this innate creativity is everywhere. In the fact that you wake up every morning and make instant decisions about what to eat, what to wear, what to do. In the fact that you're able to read and absorb what you're hearing in this book. In the fact that you have made things, that you have earned money, that you have relationships and a place to live.

And just to be clear, I'm not talking about working harder to create a new life for yourself. It's actually the opposite. It's about allowing the natural flow of life to carry you along. If you feel like you're paddling upstream, stop. If you feel like you're exerting a lot of effort, stop. If you feel like you're working really, really hard to make something happen, stop. None of that exertion and stress is necessary or helpful, and it's not how we are designed to live, anyway.

Creating this new life with the gift of permission is natural and easy, not difficult or stressful or filled with hard and grueling work.

You Have Permission: How to Stop Doing Stuff You Don't Want to Do and Start Doing Stuff You Do Want to Do

And while we're on the subject, please stop "working on yourself." (Do you know how many years of my life I spent doing that? Ugh!) There is nothing – absolutely nothing – about you that needs to be fixed, changed or improved upon. Any thoughts you have that tell you otherwise? You have permission to ignore them. They'll come back around, but the more you simply allow them to be there and not engage with them, the more of that innate creativity and freedom you'll begin to experience on a daily basis.

You have something, or several "somethings," that the world will be richer for having experienced, through your unique ability to bring it to us. You also have everything you need to bring those "somethings" to life.

I am really excited to see what happens for you as you give yourself permission to do what you want to do, and to stop doing what you don't want to do.

It's time for you to live the life you were meant to live.

You have permission ...

To stop listening to your thinking (because it's not telling you the truth, and it's not who you are).

To stop believing that your feelings can tell you anything about the future or about the quality of your life (they're only reflecting momentary thinking, and that's all they ever do).

To stop feeling chronically stressed, because stress is coming from thoughts that you're not obligated to listen to.

To stop worrying about everyone and everything, including yourself.

To take a break from what is troubling you.

You have permission ...

To dream without worrying about whether it will happen.

To relax (really).

To spend time alone when you want to.

To unplug.

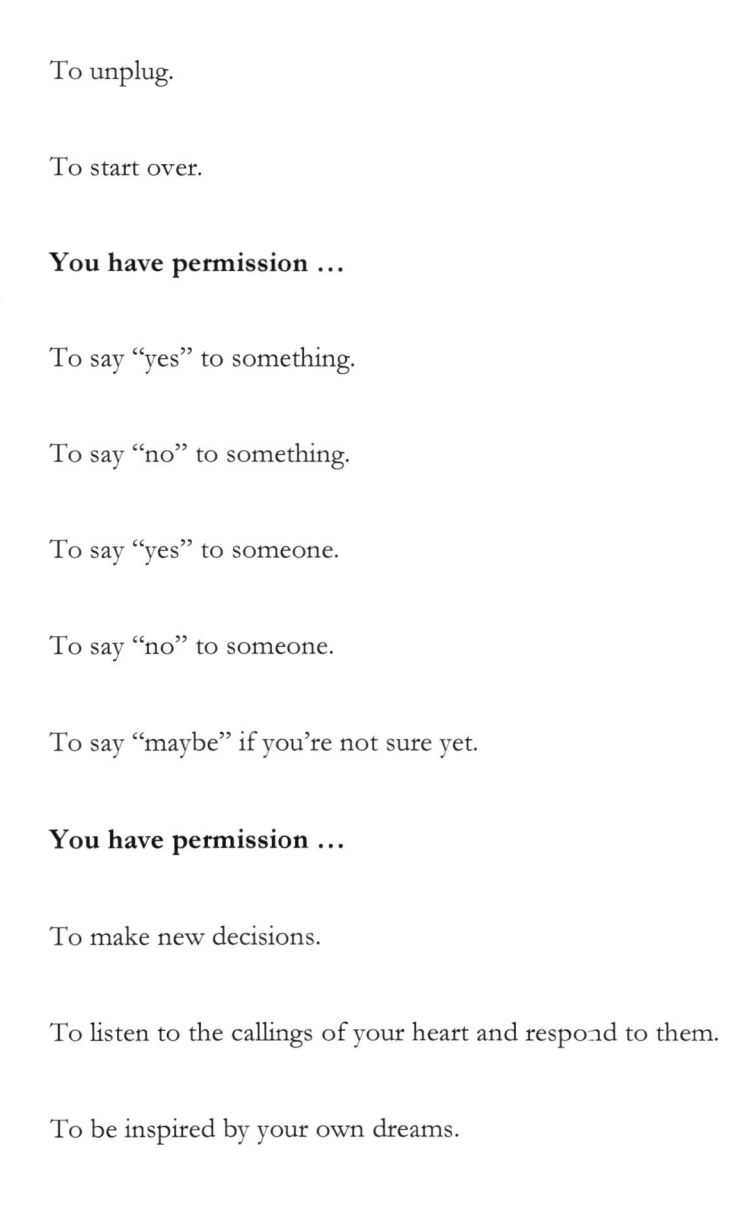

To start over.

You have permission ...

To say "yes" to something.

To say "no" to something.

To say "yes" to someone.

To say "no" to someone.

To say "maybe" if you're not sure yet.

You have permission ...

To make new decisions.

To listen to the callings of your heart and respond to them.

To be inspired by your own dreams.

To be different.

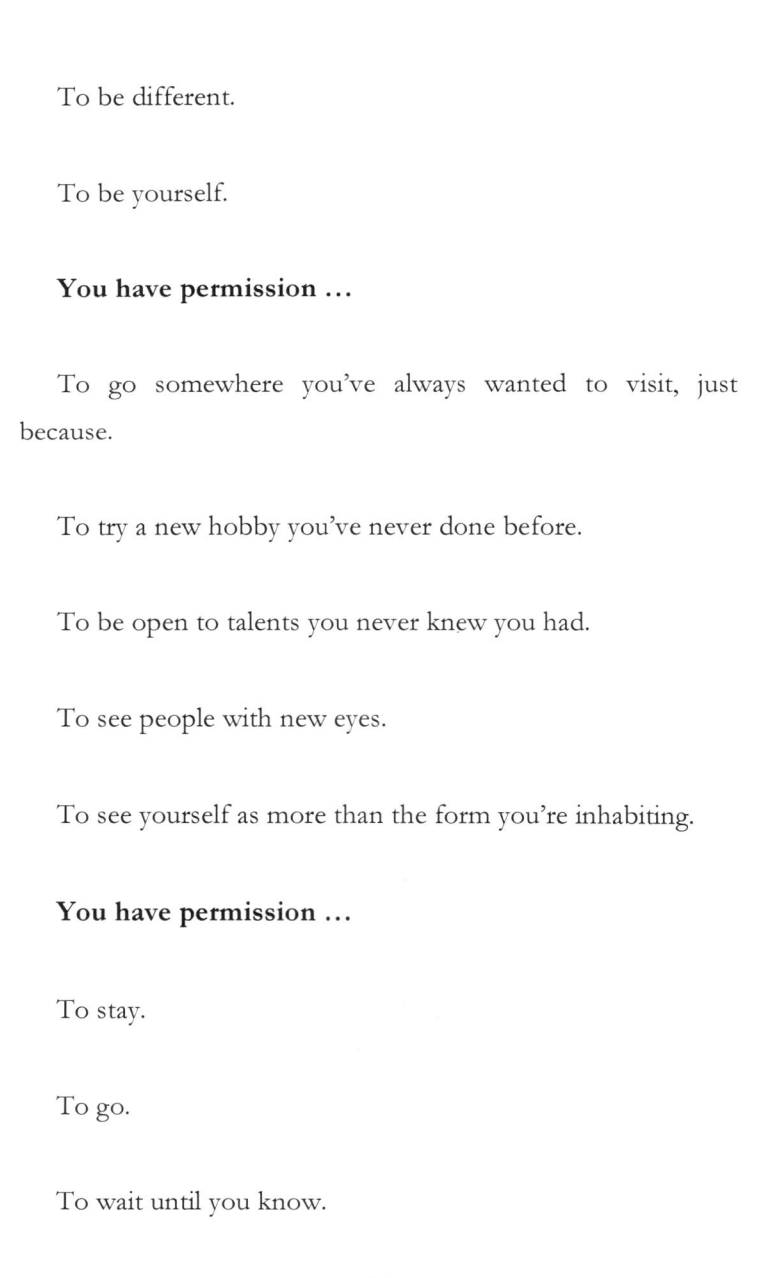

To be yourself.

You have permission …

To go somewhere you've always wanted to visit, just because.

To try a new hobby you've never done before.

To be open to talents you never knew you had.

To see people with new eyes.

To see yourself as more than the form you're inhabiting.

You have permission …

To stay.

To go.

To wait until you know.

To do something.

To do nothing.

You have permission ...

To stop doing things you don't want to do anymore.

To start doing things you do want to do.

To wake up tomorrow and do anything.

To answer what is calling to you.

To relax into your infinite and innate creativity — and allow it to help you live the life of your dreams.

Pause for Reflection

- So ... what do you want to stop doing? And what do you want to do?
- Who else in your life can you grant permission to? Give them this gift. Go tell them they have permission. Today.

Chapter 9:
Tell Me All About It

I would love to hear what changes happen in your life, now that you've given yourself permission.

1) Your review of this short book on Amazon would be so appreciated. Thank you.

2) If this book has been valuable to you, please share it on social media, or give a copy to a friend or loved one. You might find people in your workplace, your neighborhood, your place of worship or your child's school who could benefit, too.

3) Tweet @MaryJSchiller and share your experience of giving yourself – and someone else in your life that you care about (because lots of people need it!) – permission.

4) Subscribe online at www.maryschiller.com to learn more about upcoming books, classes, workshops and personalized coaching. I want you to live the life of your dreams, starting right now. You can also contact me directly via my website.

Thank you for reading and sharing *You Have Permission: How to stop doing stuff you <u>don't</u> want to do and start doing stuff you <u>do</u> want to do.* I really appreciate it.

Much love to you,
Mary

The End … of Doing Stuff You Don't Want to Do and the Start of Doing Stuff You Do Want to Do

About the Author

Mary Schiller is an author and coach who helps people experience more joy, relaxation, creativity and clarity.

She is also the author of *The Joy Formula: The simple equation that will change your life*; *Mind Yoga: The simple solution to stress that you've never heard before*; and *A-ha! How to solve any problem in record time*. More books to come, too.

Before she began coaching people and writing books, Mary was a journalist and also taught university students how to write the perfect essay. Later, she became a communications officer at an Ivy League university, and she holds advanced degrees in English and in education.

A native Californian, Mary loves the sun and the surf but also enjoys traveling. She's passionate about classical music (Beethoven is unmatched), art, photography and knitting, particularly sweaters. She's married and has a grown daughter plus two adorable cats. While Mary and her husband currently live in California, they may be making a move across the Atlantic very soon. Wherever she may be, you can find and connect with Mary online at www.maryschiller.com.

18645603R00040

Printed in Poland
by Amazon Fulfillment
Poland Sp. z o.o., Wrocław